Born in 1951

By

Kerry Butters.

Born in 1951

Millennium:	2nd millennium
Centuries:	19th century – **20th century** – 21st century

1951 (MCMLI) was a common year starting on Monday (dominical letter G) of the Gregorian calendar, the 1951st year of the Common Era (CE) and *Anno Domini* (AD) designations, the 951st year of the 2nd millennium, the 51st year of the 20th century, and the 2nd year of the 1950s decade.

Contents

Events

January

- January 1 – First week as No. 1 single on *Billboard* and *Cashbox* charts in the United States of Patti Page hit song "Tennessee Waltz".
- January 4 – Korean War: Third Battle of Seoul: Chinese and North Korean forces capture Seoul for the second time (they had lost Seoul in the Second Battle of Seoul in September 1950).
- January 9 – The Government of the United Kingdom announces abandonment of the Tanganyika groundnut scheme for the cultivation of peanuts in the Tanganyika Territory with the writing off of £36.5M debt.
- January 15 – In a court in West Germany, Ilse Koch, The "Witch of Buchenwald", wife of the commandant

of the Buchenwald concentration camp, is sentenced to life imprisonment.

- January 20 – Avalanches in the Alps kill 240 and bury 45,000 for a time in Switzerland, Austria and Italy.
- January 25 – Dutch author Anne de Vries releases the first volume of her novel *Journey Through the Night* (*Reis door de nacht*) set during World War II.
- January 27 – Nuclear testing at the Nevada Test Site begins with a 1-kiloton bomb dropped on Frenchman Flat, northwest of Las Vegas.

February

- February – Convention People's Party wins national elections in Gold Coast (British colony).
- February 1 – The United Nations General Assembly declares that China is an aggressor in the Korean War in United Nations General Assembly Resolution 498.
- February 4–February 8 – Surgeons remove an ovarian cyst from Gertrude Levandowski in a 96-hour long operation in Chicago. She loses almost half of her weight and emerges weighing 140 kg.
- February 6 – A Pennsylvania Railroad passenger train derails near Woodbridge Township, New Jersey, killing 85 people and injuring over 500, in one of the worst rail disasters in American history.

- February 12 – Muhammad Reza Shah marries Soraya Esfandiary-Bakhtiari.
- February 15 – Start of the 1951 New Zealand waterfront dispute, which lasts for 151 days.
- February 19 – Jean Lee becomes the last woman hanged in Australia, when Lee and her 2 pimps are hanged for the murder and torture of a 73-year-old bookmaker.
- February 27 – The Twenty-second Amendment to the United States Constitution, limiting Presidents to two terms, is ratified.

March

March 29: The Rosenbergs sentenced to death.

March 31: Remington Rand delivers the first UNIVAC I computer.

- March 2 – The first NBA All-Star Game of basketball is played in the Boston Garden.
- March 3 or 5 – Jackie Brenston "and His Delta Cats" (actually Ike Turner's Kings of Rhythm) record "Rocket 88" at Sam Phillips' Sun Studio in Memphis, Tennessee, a candidate for the first rock and roll record (released in April). It is covered on June 14 by Bill Haley and His Saddlemen.
- March 6 – The trial of Julius and Ethel Rosenberg for conspiracy to commit espionage begins in the United States.
- March 9 – United Artists releases sci-fi film *The Man from Planet X* in the United States.
- March 12 – Hank Ketcham's best-selling comic strip *Dennis the Menace* appears in newspapers across the United States for the first time.

- March 14
  - Korean War: For the second time, United Nations troops recapture Seoul during Operation Ripper.
  - West Germany joins UNESCO.
- March 29
  - Second Red Scare: Julius and Ethel Rosenberg are convicted of conspiracy to commit espionage. On April 5 they are sentenced to receive the death penalty.
  - Rodgers and Hammerstein's *The King and I* opens on Broadway and runs for three years. It is the first of their musicals specifically written for an actress (Gertrude Lawrence). Lawrence is stricken with cancer during the run of the show and dies halfway through its run a year later. The show makes a star of Yul Brynner.
  - The 23rd Academy Awards ceremony is held; *All About Eve* wins the Best Picture award and four others.
- March 31 – Remington Rand delivers the first UNIVAC I computer to the United States Census Bureau.

April

- April 5–13 – The most complete recording of George Gershwin's opera *Porgy and Bess* up to

- April 11
  - U.S. President Harry S. Truman relieves General Douglas MacArthur of his Far Eastern commands.
  - After its removal from Westminster Abbey on Christmas Day, 1950, the Stone of Scone resurfaces on the altar of Arbroath Abbey.
- April 18 – The Treaty of Paris (1951) is adopted, establishing the European Coal and Steel Community.
- April 21 – The National Olympic Committee of the Soviet Union is formed. The USSR first participates in the Olympic Games at Helsinki, Finland, in 1952.
- April 24 – In Yokohama, Japan, a fire on a train kills more than 100.
- April 28 – Robert Menzies' Liberal Party government in Australia is re-elected for a second term.
- April 29 – RKO releases the Howard Hawks sci-fi film, *The Thing (From Another World)*.

May

- May 1 – The opera house of Geneva, Switzerland is almost destroyed in a fire.
- May 3
  - King George VI opens London's Royal Festival Hall as a patron.
  - The Festival of Britain opens.

- The U.S. Senate Committee on Armed Services and U.S. Senate Committee on Foreign Relations begins its closed door hearings into the dismissal of General Douglas MacArthur by U.S. President Harry S Truman.
- May 9 – Operation Greenhouse: The first thermonuclear weapon is tested on Enewetok Atoll in the Marshall Islands, by the United States.
- May 14 – The first volunteer-run passenger trains run on Talyllyn Railway, Wales.
- May 15 – A military coup occurs in Bolivia.
- May 21 – The 9th Street Art Exhibition, otherwise known as the Ninth Street Show, a gathering of a number of notable artists, marks the stepping-out of the post war New York avant-garde, collectively known as the New York School.
- May 23 – The Tibetan government signs the Seventeen Point Agreement for the Peaceful Liberation of Tibet with the People's Republic of China.
- May 25 – The first atomic bomb "boosted" by the inclusion of thermonuclear materials, is tested in the "Item" test on Enewetok Atoll in the Marshall Islands by the United States.

- May 28 – *The Goon Show* is first broadcast on BBC Home Service in the U.K.; the first series was entitled "Crazy People".

June

- June 4 – Foley Square trial concludes review in U.S. Supreme Court as Dennis v. United States, with a ruling against the defendants (overturned by Yates v. United States in 1957)
- June 14 – UNIVAC I is dedicated by the U.S. Census Bureau.
- June 15–July 1– In New Mexico, Arizona, California, Oregon, Washington and British Columbia, thousands of acres of forests are destroyed in fires.

July

- July 1
  - Colombo Plan operations commence.
  - Judy Garland opens the first of 14 concerts in Dublin, Ireland at the Theatre Royal.
- July 5 – William Shockley, John Bardeen and Walter Brattain announce the invention of the junction transistor.
- July 10 – Korean War: Armistice negotiations begin at Kaesong.
- July 13

- The Great Flood of 1951 reaches its highest point in northeast Kansas, culminating in the greatest flood damage to date in the Midwestern United States.
- MGM's Technicolor film version of *Show Boat*, starring Kathryn Grayson, Ava Gardner and Howard Keel, premieres at Radio City Music Hall in New York City. The musical brings overnight fame to bass-baritone William Warfield (who sings *Ol' Man River* in the film).
- July 14 – In Joplin, Missouri, the George Washington Carver National Monument becomes the first United States National Monument to honor an African American.
- July 16 – King Léopold III of Belgium abdicates in favour of his son Baudouin.
- July 17 – King Baudouin takes the oath as king of Belgium.
- July 20 – King Abdullah I of Jordan is assassinated by a Palestinian while attending Friday prayers in Jerusalem. He is succeeded by his son, King Talal.
- July 26 – Walt Disney's 13th animated film, *Alice in Wonderland*, premieres in London, United Kingdom.
- July 30 – David Lean's film of *Oliver Twist* is finally shown in the United States, after 10 minutes of supposedly anti-Semitic references and closeups of

Alec Guinness as Fagin are cut. It will not be shown uncut in the U.S. until 1970.

August

- August 11 – René Pleven becomes Prime Minister of France.
- August 12 – J. D. Salinger's coming-of-age story *The Catcher in the Rye* is first published in the United States.
- August 31 – The first Volkswagen Beetle rolls off the plant in Uitenhage, South Africa.

September

- September 1 – The United States, Australia and New Zealand all sign a mutual defense pact, called the ANZUS Treaty.
- September 3 – The American soap opera *Search for Tomorrow* debuts on CBS.
- September 8
  - Treaty of San Francisco: In San Francisco, 48 representatives out of 51 attending sign a peace treaty with Japan to formally end the Pacific War; the delegations of the Soviet Union, Poland and Czechoslovakia do not sign the treaty instead favoring separate treaties.

- Japan-U.S. Security Treaty, which allows United States Armed Forces being stationed in Japan after the occupation of Japan, is signed by Japan and the United States.
- September 9 – Chinese communist forces move into Lhasa, the capital of Tibet.
- September 10 – The United Kingdom begins an economic boycott of Iran.
- September 18 – Tennessee Williams's adaptation of *A Streetcar Named Desire* premieres, becoming a critical and box-office smash.
- September 20 – NATO accepts Greece and Turkey as members.
- September 24 – MGM releases the musical *Show Boat*.
- September 26–September 28 – A blue sun is seen over Europe: the effect is due to ash coming from the Canadian forest fires 4 months previously.
- September 28 – 20th Century Fox releases the Robert Wise science fiction film, *The Day the Earth Stood Still*.

October

- October 3 – "Shot Heard 'Round the World": One of the greatest moments in Major League Baseball history occurs when the New York Giants' Bobby Thomson hits a game-winning home run in the bottom of the 9th inning off of Brooklyn Dodgers pitcher Ralph Branca, to win the National League pennant after being down 14 games.

- October 4
  - MGM's Technicolor musical film, *An American in Paris*, starring Gene Kelly and Leslie Caron, premieres in New York. It was directed by Vincente Minnelli. It would go on to win 6 Academy Awards, including Best Picture.
  - Shoppers World (one of the first shopping malls in the U.S.) opens in Framingham, Massachusetts.
- October 6 – Malayan Emergency: Communist insurgents kill British commander Sir Henry Gurney.
- October 14 – Organization of Central American States (*Organización de Estados Centroamericanos*, ODECA) formed.
- October 15
  - Norethisterone, the progestin used in the combined oral contraceptive pill, is synthesized by Luis E. Miramontes in Mexico.
  - *I Love Lucy* makes its television debut on CBS in the United States.
- October 16
  - Judy Garland begins a series of concerts in New York's Palace Theatre.

- Prime Minister Liaquat Ali Khan of Pakistan is assassinated.
- East China Normal University is founded in Shanghai, China.
- October 17 – CBS's Eye logo premieres on American television.
- October 19 – The state of war between the United States and Germany is officially ended.
- October 20 – The Johnny Bright incident occurs in Stillwater, Oklahoma.
- October 21 – A storm in southern Italy kills over 100.
- October 24 – U.S. President Harry Truman declares an official end to war with Germany.
- October 26 – Winston Churchill is re-elected Prime Minister of the United Kingdom (a month before his 77th birthday) in a general election which sees the defeat of Clement Attlee's Labour government after six years in power.
- October 27 – Farouk of Egypt declares himself king of Sudan, with no support.
- October 31 – The film *Scrooge*, starring Alastair Sim, opens in England.

November

- November 1 – The first military exercises for nuclear war, with infantry troops included, are held in the Nevada desert.
- November 10 – Direct dial coast-to-coast telephone service begins in the United States.
- November 11
  - Juan Perón is re-elected president of Argentina.
  - Monogram Pictures releases sci-fi film *Flight to Mars* in the United States.
- November 12 – The National Ballet of Canada performs for the first time in Eaton Auditorium, Toronto.
- November 20 – The Po (river) floods in northern Italy.
- November 22 – Paramount Pictures releases George Pal science fiction film *When Worlds Collide* in the United States.
- November 24 – The Broadway play *Gigi* opens, starring Audrey Hepburn as the lead character.
- November 28 – The U.K. film *Scrooge*, starring Alastair Sim, premieres in the United States under the title of Charles Dickens's original novel, *A Christmas Carol*.
- November 29 – LEO (computer) runs the worlds first commercial computer program, Bakery Valuations, for J. Lyons and Co.'s tea shops in the U.K.

December

- c. December – The Institute of War and Peace Studies is established by Dwight D. Eisenhower at Columbia University in New York (of which he is President) with William T. R. Fox as first director.
- December 3 – The Lebanese University is founded in Lebanon.
- December 5 – Provisional Intergovernmental Committee for the Movement of Migrants from Europe.
- December 6 – A state of emergency is declared in Egypt due to increasing riots.
- December 13 – A water storage tank collapses in Tucumcari, New Mexico, resulting in 4 deaths and 200 buildings destroyed.
- December 16 – Salar Jung Museum is opened to the public by Prime Minister of India Jawaharlal Nehru.
- December 17 – "We Charge Genocide", a petition describing genocide against African Americans, is delivered to the United Nations.
- December 20
  - Experimental Breeder Reactor I (EBR-1), the world's first (experimental) nuclear power plant, opens in Idaho.

- A chartered Curtiss C-46 Commando crash-lands in Cobourg, Ontario Canada; all on board survive.
- The World Meteorological Organization becomes a specialized agency of the United Nations.
- December 22 – The Selangor Labour Party is founded in Selangor, Malaya.
- December 23 – John Huston's drama film *The African Queen*, starring Humphrey Bogart and Katharine Hepburn, premieres in Hollywood.
- December 24
  - Libya becomes independent from Italy.
  - Gian Carlo Menotti's 45-minute opera, *Amahl and the Night Visitors*, premieres live on NBC in the United States, becoming the first opera written especially for television.
- December 31 – The Marshall Plan expires after distributing more than $13.3 billion US in foreign aid to rebuild Europe.

Unknown dates

- A fourth and final forest fire starts in the Tillamook Burn, Oregon; but unlike earlier fires this one burns only 32,700 acres (132 km²), and within an area already affected by the earlier fires.

- A research team publishes the *Interlingua–English Dictionary*.
- IBM (United Kingdom) is formed.
- In Munich, Germany, a collection of mementos and personal papers belonging to Adolf Hitler are turned over to Bayerische Landesbank for authentication and eventual sale. Among the documents are his *appointment as Chancellor* signed by President Paul von Hindenburg, his *Austrian passport,* as well as an assortment of swastika insignia pins and medals. An initial offer of $200,000.00 is made for the collection.
- Stockholm, Sweden – An 18-year-old sailor is fined for kissing in public. The court calls his actions "obnoxious behavior repulsive to the public morals."
- The United States becomes malaria-free (excluding territories and possessions)

Births

January

Kirstie Alley

Phil Collins

Blaise Compaore

Gordon Brown

Dave Benton

- January 1 – Ashfaq Hussain, Urdu poet

- January 2 – Waldir Peres, Brazilian footballer
- January 5 – Steve Arnold, English footballer
- January 6 – Kim Wilson, American singer and harmonica player
- January 8
  - Kenny Anthony, Prime Minister of Saint Lucia
  - John McTiernan, American director, producer and writer
- January 12
  - Kirstie Alley, American actress
  - Rush Limbaugh, American conservative radio personality
- January 20 – Ian Hill, English rock bassist (Judas Priest)
- January 25 – Steve Prefontaine, American runner (d. 1975)
- January 30 – Phil Collins, English rock musician and producer
- January 31
  - Dave Benton, Aruban-American singer, Eurovision Song Contest 2001 winner
  - Harry Wayne Casey, American musician, songwriter and producer
  - Phil Manzanera, British rock musician

February

- February 1 – Albert Salvadó, Andorran writer
- February 3
  - Blaise Compaoré, President of Burkina Faso (1987-2014)
  - Felipe Muñoz, Mexican swimmer
  - Eugenijus Riabovas, Lithuanian football manager
- February 5 – Ryūsei Nakao, Japanese actor, singer and voice actor
- February 13 – David Naughton, American actor
- February 14 – Kevin Keegan, English footballer and football manager
- February 15
  - Melissa Manchester, American pop singer
  - Jane Seymour, English actress
- February 16
  - Mike Flanagan, American baseball pitcher
  - William Katt, American film and television actor
- February 19 – Muhammad Tahir-ul-Qadri, Pakistani Islamic Sufi scholar and leader
- February 20
  - Edward Albert, American actor (d. 2006)
  - Gordon Brown, Prime Minister of the United Kingdom (2007–10)
- February 22 – Ellen Greene, American actress
- February 23 – Patricia Richardson, American actress

- February 24 – Debra Jo Rupp, American actress
- February 25 – Don Quarrie, Jamaican sprinter
- February 27 – Steve Harley, British rock musician

March

Chris Rea

Kurt Russell

- March 1
  - Sergei Kourdakov, KGB agent

- o Mike Read, British television presenter and radio disc jockey
- March 3 – Heizō Takenaka, Japanese economist
- March 4
  - o Edelgard Bulmahn, German politician
  - o Kenny Dalglish, Scottish footballer and football manager
  - o Mike Quarry, American light-heavyweight boxer (d. 2006)
  - o Chris Rea, British singer and musician
  - o Gwen Welles, American actress (d. 1993)
  - o Linda Yamamoto, Japanese pop star
- March 6 – Gerrie Knetemann, Dutch cyclist (d. 2004)
- March 8 – Karen Kain, Canadian ballerina
- March 12 – Susan Musgrave, Canadian poet and children's writer
- March 13 – Charo, Spanish-American singer and entertainer
- March 14 – Jerry Greenfield, American co-founder of *Ben & Jerry's* ice cream
- March 17 – Kurt Russell, American actor
- March 18 – Ben Cohen, American co-founder of *Ben & Jerry's* ice cream
- March 19 – Fred Berry, American actor (d. 2003)
- March 24 – Tommy Hilfiger, American fashion designer

- March 26 – Carl Wieman, American physicist, Nobel Prize laureate
- March 30 – Wolfgang Niedecken, German singer

April

Dale Earnhardt

- April 5
  - Joe Bowen, Canadian hockey broadcaster
  - Dean Kamen, American inventor and entrepreneur
  - Frank Moulaert, Flemish scholar
  - Guy Vanderhaeghe, Canadian author
- April 6 – Bert Blyleven, Dutch Major League Baseball player
- April 7 – Janis Ian, American singer and songwriter
- April 8
  - Geir Haarde, Prime Minister of Iceland (2006–2009)

- Joan Sebastian, Mexican singer-songwriter (d. 2015)
- April 10 – David Helvarg, American journalist and activist
- April 11 – Doris Angleton, American socialite and murder victim (d. 1997)
- April 12 – Tom Noonan, American actor
- April 13
    - Peabo Bryson, American singer
    - Peter Davison, British actor
    - Max Weinberg, American drummer
- April 14 – Julian Lloyd Webber, English cellist
- April 16
    - Mordechai Ben David, American singer
    - Ioan Mihai Cochinescu, Romanian writer
    - Björgvin Halldórsson, Icelandic singer
    - Pierre Toutain-Dorbec, French photographer
- April 17
    - Horst Hrubesch, German football player
    - Olivia Hussey, Argentine-born actress (*Romeo and Juliet*)
- April 19 – Jóannes Eidesgaard, Prime Minister of the Faroe Islands
- April 20
    - Louise Jameson, British actress

- o Luther Vandross, American R&B/soul musician (d. 2005)
- April 21 – Tony Danza, American actor and comedian
- April 23 – Allison Krause, Kent State University shooting victim (d. 1970).
- April 27 – Ace Frehley, original guitarist of Kiss
- April 29 – Dale Earnhardt, American race-car driver (d. 2001)

May

Anatoly Karpov

Antonis Samaras

- May 3 – Christopher Cross, American singer-songwriter
- May 4 – Jackie Jackson, American singer
- May 6
    - Antonio Saldías, Chilean historian
    - Samuel Doe, President of Liberia (d. 1990)
- May 9
    - Christopher Dewdney, Canadian poet
    - Joy Harjo, Native American poet
- May 13
    - Sharon Sayles Belton, Mayor of Minneapolis, Minnesota
    - Jumbo Tsuruta, Japanese professional wrestler (d. 2000)
- May 15
    - Yoshifumi Hibako, Japanese general
    - Jonathan Richman, American musician
    - Frank Wilczek, American physicist, Nobel Prize laureate
- May 16 – Unshō Ishizuka, Japanese voice actor
- May 19
    - Al Franken, American comedian turned politician (United States Senator, D-MN)
    - Joey Ramone, American rock musician (Ramones) (d. 2001)
    - Dick Slater, American professional wrestler

- May 23
  - Anatoly Karpov, Russian chess player
  - Antonis Samaras, Greek economist and politician, 185th Prime Minister of Greece
- May 26
  - Madeleine Taylor-Quinn, Irish politician
  - Sally Ride, American astronaut (d. 2012)
- May 30
  - Stephen Tobolowsky, American actor
  - Fernando Lugo, President of Paraguay

June

Bonnie Tyler

Stellan Skarsgård

Mary McAleese

- June 2 – Larry Robinson, Canadian hockey player
- June 5 – Suze Orman, American financial advisor, writer and television personality
- June 8 – Bonnie Tyler, Welsh singer
- June 12
    - Brad Delp, American rock vocalist (Boston) (d. 2007)
    - Andranik Margaryan, 14th Prime Minister of Armenia (d. 2007)
- June 13
    - Stellan Skarsgård, Swedish actor
    - Richard Thomas, American actor
- June 14 – Paul Boateng, British politician
- June 15 – Álvaro Colom Caballeros, Current President of Guatemala
- June 16 – Roberto Durán, Panamanian boxer
- June 18 – Gyula Sax, Hungarian chess grandmaster (d. 2014)
- June 20

- ○ Tress MacNeille, American voice actress
- ○ Paul Muldoon, Irish poet
- June 21 – Nils Lofgren, American musician
- June 24 – David Rodigan, British radio DJ/actor
- June 27
  - ○ Julia Duffy, American actress
  - ○ Mary McAleese, 8th President of Ireland
- June 28
  - ○ Lloyd Maines, American musician and record producer
  - ○ Lalla Ward, British actress
- June 29 – Keno Don Rosa, American comic book author
- June 30 – Stanley Clarke, American bassist

July

Geoffrey Rush

Anjelica Huston

Chris Cooper

Elio Di Rupo

Robin Williams

Dana Rosemary Scallon

- July 1
    - Anne Feeney, American folk singer
    - Terrence Mann, American actor and dancer
- July 2
    - Elisabeth Brooks, Canadian actress (d. 1997)
    - Sylvia Rivera, American transgender activist (d. 2002)
- July 3 – Richard Hadlee, New Zealand cricketer
- July 5 – Goose Gossage, American baseball player
- July 6 – Geoffrey Rush, Australian actor
- July 8 – Anjelica Huston, American actress
- July 9 – Chris Cooper, American actor
- July 10 – Cheryl Wheeler, American singer and songwriter
- July 12 – Cheryl Ladd, American actress and singer
- July 14 – Erich Hallhuber, German actor (d. 2003)
- July 16 – Jean-Luc Mongrain, Canadian news anchor and journalist
- July 18 – Elio Di Rupo, Belgian politician

- July 21 – Robin Williams, American actor and comedian (d. 2014)
- July 23
  - Edie McClurg, American actress
  - Michael McConnohie, American actor
- July 24
  - Lynda Carter, American actress and singer
  - Chris Smith, British politician
- July 25 – Yury Kovalchuk, Russian oligarch
- July 26 – Sabine Leutheusser-Schnarrenberger, German politician
- July 28
  - Doug Collins, American basketball player, coach and analyst
  - Garrett Hongo, American poet
- July 31
  - Evonne Goolagong Cawley, Australian tennis player
  - Vjekoslav Šutej, Croatian orchestra conductor

August

- August 2 – Andrew Gold, American singer-songwriter and musician (10cc, Wax) (d. 2011)
- August 3 – Jay North, American actor
- August 3 – Marcel Dionne, Canadian hockey player
- August 6

- Catherine Hicks, American actress
- Daryl Somers, Australian television personality
- August 8
  - Louis van Gaal, Dutch football player and manager
  - Mamoru Oshii, Japanese film director
  - Randy Shilts, American journalist and author (d. 1994)
- August 11 – Katsumi Chō, Japanese voice actor
- August 12 – Willie Horton, American criminal
- August 13 – Dan Fogelberg, American singer, songwriter and multi-instrumentalist (d. 2007)
- August 14 – Carl Lumbly, American actor
- August 15 – Jim Allen, West Indian cricketer
- August 17 – Richard Hunt, American puppeteer (d. 1992)
- August 19 – John Deacon, English rock bassist
- August 20 – Greg Bear, American author
- August 21
  - Eric Goles, Chilean mathematician and computer scientist
  - Chesley V. Morton, American politician and securities arbitrator
- August 22 – Chandra Prakash Mainali, Nepalese politician
- August 23

- Mark Hudson, American musician
- Akhmad Kadyrov, President of Chechnya (d. 2004)
- Queen Noor of Jordan, born Lisa Najeeb Halaby, American-born queen consort
- Jimi Jamison, American musician (d. 2014)

- August 24 – Orson Scott Card, American writer

Rob Halford

- August 25 – Rob Halford, English rock singer
- August 26 – Edward Witten, American mathematician and Fields medalist
- August 27 – Mack Brown, American college football coach
- August 28 – Wayne Osmond, American pop singer
- August 30 – Dana Rosemary Scallon, Irish singer, Eurovision Song Contest 1970 winner and Member of the European Parliament (MEP).

September

Michael Keaton

David Coverdale

Mark Hamill

Michelle Bachelet

- September 2
    - Jim DeMint, American politician, United States Senator (R-SC)
    - Mark Harmon, American actor
- September 5 – Michael Keaton, American actor
- September 7
    - Chrissie Hynde, American rock singer
    - Bert Jones, American football player
- September 11 – Mr. Butch, American homeless person and Boston icon (d. 2007)
- September 12
    - Bertie Ahern, Taoiseach of Ireland
    - Joe Pantoliano, American actor
- September 13
    - Jean Smart, American actress (*Designing Women*)
    - Linda Wong, American porn star (d. 1987)
- September 15
    - Pete Carroll, football coach

- Fred Seibert, American producer and Frederator Studios founder
- September 17 – Cassandra Peterson, American actress (*Elvira, Mistress of the Dark*)
- September 18
    - Dee Dee Ramone, American musician (d. 2002)
    - Darryl Stingley, American football player for the NFL New England Patriots (d. 2007)
- September 21 – Aslan Maskhadov, President of Chechnya (d. 2005)
- September 22
    - David Coverdale, English singer and musician
    - Wolfgang Petry, German singer
- September 25
    - Pedro Almodóvar, Spanish filmmaker
    - Mark Hamill, American actor (*Star Wars*)
- September 26 – Stuart Tosh, Scottish musician
- September 27 – Paul Craig, English professor of law
- September 28 – Jim Diamond, Scottish singer-songwriter (d. 2015)
- September 29
    - Michelle Bachelet, President of Chile
    - Andrés Caicedo, Colombian writer (d. 1977)
    - Maureen Caird, Australian hurdler
    - Mike Enriquez, Filipino radio and television newscaster

- September 30 – Barry Marshall, Australian physician and recipient of the Nobel Prize in Physiology or Medicine

October

Sting

- October 2 – Sting, British singer, rock musician, philanthropist
- October 3
  - Bernard Cooper, American writer
  - Keb' Mo', American musician
  - Dave Winfield, baseball player
- October 4 – Bakhytzhan Kanapyanov, Kazakh poet
- October 5 – Bob Geldof, Irish musician (The Boomtown Rats)
- October 6 – Manfred Winkelhock, German race car driver
- October 7 – John Mellencamp, American musician and songwriter

- October 10 – Epeli Ganilau, Fijian soldier and statesman
- October 11
  - Jean-Jacques Goldman, French singer and songwriter
  - Jon Miller, American sports announcer
- October 15 – Rafael Vaganian, Armenian chess grandmaster
- October 18
  - Mike Antonovich, American ice hockey player and executive
  - Terry McMillan, American author
- October 22 – William David Sanders, American victim of the Columbine High School massacre (d. 1999)
- October 23 – Charly García, Argentine musician and songwriter
- October 25 – Richard Lloyd, American rock guitarist
- October 26
  - Willie P. Bennett, Canadian songwriter and singer (d. 2008)
  - Bootsy Collins, American musician, singer-songwriter
- October 27 – Éric Morena, French singer
- October 30 – Harry Hamlin, American actor

November

Traian Băsescu

Kathryn Bigelow

- November 2 – Thomas Mallon, American author and critic
- November 3 – Ed Murawinski, American cartoonist (*New York Daily News*)
- November 4 – Traian Băsescu, President of Romania
- November 9 – Lou Ferrigno, American actor and bodybuilder
- November 10 – Danilo Medina, President of the Dominican Republic

- November 11 – Marc Summers, American television host
- November 14 – Jacob ter Veldhuis, Dutch composer
- November 15 – Alamgir Hashmi, English poet
  - Beverly D'Angelo, American actress
- November 16
  - Miguel Sandoval, American actor
  - Paula Vogel, American playwright
- November 18 – Justin Raimondo, American author
- November 19 – Lord Falconer of Thoroton, British politician
- November 20 – Rodger Bumpass voice actor notably Squidward
- November 21 – Thomas Roth, German news anchor presenter and television presenter
- November 24 – Chet Edwards, American politician
- November 26 – Cicciolina, Hungarian-Italian actress and politician
- November 27 – Teri DeSario, American singer-songwriter
- November 29
  - Kathryn Bigelow, American film director
  - Roger Troutman, American funk musician (d. 1999)
- November 30 – Christian Bernard, French-born mystic

December

- December 1
  - Sherry Aldridge, American singer
  - Obba Babatundé, American actor
  - Jaco Pastorius, American bassist (d. 1987)
  - Treat Williams, American actor
- December 2 – Adrian Devine, American baseball pitcher
- December 3
  - Natalis Chan, Hong Kong actor and producer
  - Riki Choshu, Korean-Japanese professional wrestler
- December 4
  - Chang Fei, Taiwanese TV personality
  - Patricia Wettig, American actress
- December 6 – Tomson Highway, Canadian writer
- December 8
  - Bill Bryson, American-born British author
  - Jan Eggum, Norwegian singer and songwriter
- December 10 – Doug Allder, English footballer
- December 11 – Peter T. Daniels, American scholar
- December 12 – Wau Holland, German hacker (d. 2001)
- December 14
  - Mike Krüger, German comedian and singer
  - Jan Timman, Dutch chess player

- December 17 – Ken Hitchcock, Canadian hockey coach
- December 20 – Peter May, Scottish novelist and television dramatist
- December 29 – Georges Thurston, Canadian singer (d. 2007)
- December 31 – Tom Hamilton, American musician

Date unknown

- John Kindness, Irish artist
- Adriana Monti, Italian film director
- Mike Jackson, British systems scientist and consultant

Deaths

January

- January 7 – René Guénon, French-born author (b. 1886)
- January 10 – Sinclair Lewis, American writer, Nobel Prize laureate (b. 1885)
- January 12 – Albert Guay, Canadian murderer (executed) (b. 1917)
- January 18

- ○ Amy Carmichael, Irish missionary to India (b. 1867)
- ○ Jack Holt, American actor (b. 1888)
- January 21 – Yuriko Miyamoto, Japanese novelist (b. 1899)
- January 27 – Carl Gustaf Emil Mannerheim, President of Finland (b. 1867)
- January 29 – Frank Tarrant, Australian cricketer (b. 1880)
- January 30 – Ferdinand Porsche, German auto engineer (b. 1875)

February

André Gide

- February 8 – Fritz Thyssen, German businessman and industrialist (b. 1873)
- February 9 – Eddy Duchin, American pianist and bandleader (b. 1909)
- February 13 – Lloyd C. Douglas, American author (b. 1877)

- February 18 – Lyman Gilmore, American aviation pioneer (b. 1874)
- February 19 – André Gide, French writer, Nobel Prize laureate (b. 1869)
- February 12 – Choudhry Rahmat Ali, one of the founding fathers of Pakistan (b. 1895)
- February 28 – Henry W. Armstrong, American boxer and songwriter (b. 1879)

Ivor Novello

March

- March 6 – Ivor Novello, Welsh actor, musician and composer (b. 1893)
- March 10 – Kijūrō Shidehara, Prime Minister of Japan (b. 1872)
- March 11 – János Zsupánek, Slovene (Prekmurian) poet and writer (b. 1861)
- March 12 – Alfred Hugenberg, German businessman and politician (b. 1865)
- March 14 – Val Lewton, American producer and screenwriter (b. 1904)

- March 21 – Willem Mengelberg, Dutch conductor (b. 1871)
- March 25
  - Eddie Collins, American baseball player (Chicago White Sox) and a member of the MLB Hall of Fame (b. 1887)
  - Oscar Micheaux, African-American filmmaker (b. 1884)
- March 31 – Ralph Forbes, American actor (b. 1896)

April

- April 3 – Henrik Visnapuu, Estonian poet and dramatist (b. 1890)
- April 4
  - Al Christie, Canadian-born film director and producer (b. 1881)
  - George Albert Smith, president of The Church of Jesus Christ of Latter-day Saints (b. 1870)
- April 6 – Robert Broom, Scottish paleontologist (b. 1866)
- April 14 – Ernest Bevin, British labour leade1r, politician and statesman (b. 1881)
- April 19 – Frank Hopkins, American professional horseman, soldier (b. 1865)
- April 18 – Óscar Carmona, former President of Portugal (b. 1869)

- April 21 – Lambertus Johannes Toxopeus, Dutch lepidopterist (b. 1894)
- April 22 – Horace Donisthorpe, English myrmecologist (b. 1870)
- April 23 – Charles G. Dawes, Vice President of the United States, recipient of the Nobel Peace Prize (b. 1865)
- April 29 – Ludwig Wittgenstein, Austrian philosopher (b. 1889)

Homero Manzi

May

- May 3 – Homero Manzi, Argentine Tango lyricist and author (b. 1907)
- May 6 – Henri Carton de Wiart, former Prime Minister of Belgium (b. 1869)
- May 7 – Warner Baxter, American actor (b. 1889)
- May 17
  - William Birdwood, 1st Baron Birdwood, British field marshal (b. 1865)

- Empress Teimei of Japan, Empress consort of Emperor Taishō (b. 1884)
- May 24 – Thomas N. Heffron, American silent film director (b. 1872)
- May 27 – Sir Thomas Blamey, Australian field marshal (b. 1884)
- May 29 – Fanny Brice, American entertainer (b. 1891)
- May 30 – Hermann Broch, Austrian author (b. 1886)

Serge Koussevitzky

June

- June 4 – Serge Koussevitzky, Russian conductor (b. 1874)
- June 8
  - Paul Blobel, German SS officer (executed) (b. 1894)
  - Werner Braune, German SS officer (executed) (b. 19 09)
  - Erich Naumann, German SS officer (executed) (b. 1905)

- ◦ Otto Ohlendorf, German SS officer (executed) (b. 1907)
- ◦ Oswald Pohl, German SS officer (executed) (b. 1892)
- June 9 – Mayo Methot, American actress (b. 1904)
- June 11 – Takuma Nishimura, Japanese general (executed) (d. 1951)
- June 13 – Ben Chifley, Prime Minister of Australia (b. 1885)
- June 21 – Charles Dillon Perrine, American-born astronomer, discovered two moons of Jupiter (Himalia and Elara) (b. 1867)
- June 27 – David Warfield, stage actor (b. 1866)

July

Philippe Pétain

- July 2 – Ferdinand Sauerbruch, German surgeon (b. 1875)
- July 9 – Harry Heilmann, American baseball player (Detroit Tigers) and a member of the MLB Hall of Fame (b. 1894)

- July 13 – Arnold Schoenberg, Austrian composer (b. 1874)
- July 20
    - King Abdullah I of Jordan (b. 1882)
    - Crown Prince Wilhelm of Prussia (b. 1882)
- July 23
    - Robert J. Flaherty, American filmmaker (b. 1884)
    - Philippe Pétain, French World War I marshal, leader of Vichy France (b. 1856)
- July 26 – Maximilian Ritter von Pohl, German army and air force officer (b. 1893)

Bee Ho Gray

August

Robert Walker

- August 3 – Bee Ho Gray, Native American Wild West star, silent film actor and vaudeville performer (b. 1885)
- August 14 – William Randolph Hearst, American newspaper publisher (b. 1863)
- August 15 – Artur Schnabel, Austrian-born Jewish classical pianist (b. 1882)
- August 16 – Louis Jouvet, French actor and director (b. 1887)
- August 21 – Constant Lambert, British composer (b. 1905)
- August 26 – Bill Barilko, Canadian hockey player (b. 1927)
- August 28 – Robert Walker, American actor (b. 1918)

September

- September 7
  - Maria Montez, Dominican-born actress (b. 1912)
  - John French Sloan, American artist (b. 1871)
- September 9 – Gibson Gowland, English actor (b. 1877)
- September 17 – Jimmy Yancey, American pianist and composer (b. 1898)
- September 29 – Thomas Cahill, American soccer coach (b. 1864)

October

- October 4 – Henrietta Lacks, African American originator of the HeLa cell line (b. 1920)
- October 6 – Otto Fritz Meyerhof, German-born physician and biochemist (b. 1884)
- October 12 – Leon Errol, Australian-born actor and comedian (b. 1881)
- October 16 – Liaquat Ali Khan, first Prime Minister of Pakistan (b. 1896)
- October 24 – Clarence Stewart Williams, American admiral (b. 1863)
- October 28 – Mady Christians, Austrian actress (b. 1892)

November

Sigmund Romberg

- November 3 – Richard Wallace, American film director (b. 1894)
- November 5 – Reggie Walker, South African athlete (b. 1889)

- November 9 – Sigmund Romberg, Hungarian-born composer (b. 1887)
- November 13 – Nikolai Medtner, Russian pianist and composer (b. 1880)
- November 20 – Thomas Quinlan (impresario), English opera singer (b. 1881)

Shoeless Joe Jackson

- November 25 – Harry B. Liversedge, American general (b. 1894)

December

- December 5 – Shoeless Joe Jackson, American baseball player (Chicago White Sox) (b. 1889)
- December 6
  - J. Edward Bromberg, Hungarian-born character actor (b. 1903)
  - André Gobert, French tennis player (b. 1890)
  - Harold Ross, American editor (b.1892)
- December 10 – Algernon Blackwood, English writer (b. 1869)

- December 19 – Barton Yarborough, American actor (b. 1900)
- December 23 – Enrique Santos Discépolo, Argentine tango and milonga musician and composer (b. 1901)
- December 31 – Maxim Litvinov, Russian revolutionary and Soviet diplomat (b. 1876)

Nobel Prizes

- Physics – John Cockcroft and Ernest Walton
- Chemistry – Edwin McMillan and Glenn T. Seaborg
- Physiology or Medicine – Max Theiler
- Literature – Pär Lagerkvist
- Peace – Léon Jouhaux

Best selling Toys of 1951.

- Alice (from Alice in Wonderland film), Talking Eggs from Selcol with a crank-handle to make Humpty Dumpty squeak (6/9d) - about 32p...Muffin the Mule push-along toy by Kohnstam...Kiddicraft's 'Sensible' range of cot and pram toys designed by Hilary Page.

-

- A Muffin The Mule push-along toy is the best seller this year.

-

- Mr Potato Head is launched. And Jack O'dell creates the first Matchbox car.

In the News

First nuclear bomb tests at Nevada test site.

King Abdullah of Jordan assassinated on July20th in Jerusalem.

The **Festival of Britain** opens at the Royal Festival Hall.

The Great Flood of 1951 in Midwest United States.

The popular film "The Day the Earth Stood Still" debuts.

Direct dial coast-to-coast telephone service begins in the United States.

First Color Television Pictures broadcast from Empire State Building

1951 Calendar

January 1951

Sun	Mon	Tue	Wed	Thu	Fri	Sat
	1	2	3	4	5	6
7	8	9	10	11	12	13
14	15	16	17	18	19	20
21	22	23	24	25	26	27
28	29	30	31			

February 1951

Sun	Mon	Tue	Wed	Thu	Fri	Sat
				1	2	3
4	5	6	7	8	9	10
11	12	13	14	15	16	17
18	19	20	21	22	23	24
25	26	27	28			

March 1951

Sun	Mon	Tue	Wed	Thu	Fri	Sat
				1	2	3
4	5	6	7	8	9	10
11	12	13	14	15	16	17
18	19	20	21	22	23	24
25	26	27	28	29	30	31

April 1951

Sun	Mon	Tue	Wed	Thu	Fri	Sat
1	2	3	4	5	6	7
8	9	10	11	12	13	14
15	16	17	18	19	20	21
22	23	24	25	26	27	28
29	30					

May 1951

Sun	Mon	Tue	Wed	Thu	Fri	Sat
		1	2	3	4	5
6	7	8	9	10	11	12
13	14	15	16	17	18	19
20	21	22	23	24	25	26
27	28	29	30	31		

June 1951

Sun	Mon	Tue	Wed	Thu	Fri	Sat
					1	2
3	4	5	6	7	8	9
10	11	12	13	14	15	16
17	18	19	20	21	22	23
24	25	26	27	28	29	30

July 1951

Sun	Mon	Tue	Wed	Thu	Fri	Sat
1	2	3	4	5	6	7
8	9	10	11	12	13	14
15	16	17	18	19	20	21
22	23	24	25	26	27	28
29	30	31				

August 1951

Sun	Mon	Tue	Wed	Thu	Fri	Sat
			1	2	3	4
5	6	7	8	9	10	11
12	13	14	15	16	17	18
19	20	21	22	23	24	25
26	27	28	29	30	31	

September 1951

Sun	Mon	Tue	Wed	Thu	Fri	Sat
						1
2	3	4	5	6	7	8
9	10	11	12	13	14	15
16	17	18	19	20	21	22
23	24	25	26	27	28	29
30						

October 1951

Sun	Mon	Tue	Wed	Thu	Fri	Sat
	1	2	3	4	5	6
7	8	9	10	11	12	13
14	15	16	17	18	19	20
21	22	23	24	25	26	27
28	29	30	31			

November 1951

Sun	Mon	Tue	Wed	Thu	Fri	Sat
				1	2	3
4	5	6	7	8	9	10
11	12	13	14	15	16	17
18	19	20	21	22	23	24
25	26	27	28	29	30	

December 1951

Sun	Mon	Tue	Wed	Thu	Fri	Sat
						1
2	3	4	5	6	7	8
9	10	11	12	13	14	15
16	17	18	19	20	21	22
23	24	25	26	27	28	29
30	31					

www.ingramcontent.com/pod-product-compliance
Lightning Source LLC
Chambersburg PA
CBHW071119280526
45787CB00003B/1101